# Contents

| | | |
|---|---|---|
| *Preface* | | 5 |
| *Introduction* | | 6 |
| 1. | The Meaning of Numbers | 7 |
| 2. | Single Numbers | 10 |
| 3. | Compound and Karmic Numbers | 21 |
| 4. | The Destiny Number | 49 |
| 5. | The Talent Number | 58 |
| 6. | The Heart Number | 61 |
| 7. | The Birth Force Period | 70 |
| 8. | The Ultimate Number | 83 |
| 9. | The Challenge Number | 91 |
| 10. | The Personality Number | 98 |

| | | |
|---|---|---|
| 11. | The Birthday Number | 103 |
| 12. | The Name Number | 106 |
| 13. | The Habit Number | 110 |
| 14. | The Event Number | 113 |
| 15. | Opportunities and Vocations | 124 |
| 16. | Romance and Marriage | 133 |
| 17. | Numbers and Diseases | 138 |
| 18. | Numbers and Colours | 152 |

# ALL YOU WANTED TO KNOW ABOUT
# Numerology

### VIJAYA KUMAR

**New Dawn**

NEW DAWN
An imprint of Sterling Publishers (P) Ltd.
A-59 Okhla Industrial Area, Phase-II, New Delhi-110020.
Tel: 6387070, 6386209   Fax: 91-11-6383788
E-mail: ghai@nde.vsnl.net.in
www.sterlingpublishers.com

*Numerology*
© 1999, Sterling Publishers Private Limited
ISBN 81 207 2197 7

Reprint 2002, 2004

All rights are reserved. No part of this publication may be reproduced, stored in a retrieval system or transmitted, in any form or by any means, mechanical, photocopying, recording or otherwise, without prior written permission of the publisher.

*Published by* Sterling Publishers Pvt. Ltd., New Delhi-110016
*Lasertypeset by* Vikas Compographics, New Delhi-110029.
*Printed at :* Sai Early Learners (P) Ltd.

# Preface

This book is by no means an extensive study by any professional. The data provided in this book are my own interpretations of the subject, gleaned from various books, and presented from a layperson's viewpoint.

The book deals with each aspect of the study, point by point, in a simple language, and serves as a ready reckoner for those who have no time to go through heavy, indepth studies.

The publishers and I hold no responsibility for any discrepancy in the script. We would welcome suggestions or intimation of errors that come to anybody's notice.

**Vijaya Kumar**

# Introduction

We exist in a universe of vibrations, and every person in this world has a vibration characteristic to him that is distinct from others, effecting a person in his or her birth. The history of the person's life is written in the name and date of birth. The name that a person is known by since birth contains in itself the complete character and destiny from birth till death.

The science of numbers helps one in determining the past, present and future; lucky colours, days and gems; one's vocation; state of health; personality, etc.

# The Meaning of Numbers

1. Numbers 1 to 9 are basic numbers or single numbers, while those from 10 to 65 are called compound numbers.
2. According to Pythagoras, numbers 1 to 9 are used in numerology by which all our calculations are made.
3. Each double number can be reduced to a single digit by natural addition from left to right.
4. The ultimate number that accrues after addition of all numbers is

called the spirit or soul number, representing the wheel of fortune.
5. Each number has a positive effect with which the individual is blessed.
6. The negative effect of a number also prevails when two or more numbers are in conflict.
7. Each letter of the alphabet is represented by a number, as shown on page 9.
8. In this book, we deal with single, compound and karmic numbers, and numbers of destiny, talent, heart, ultimate, challenge, personality, birthday, name, habit and event.

# Letters and Their Numerical Values

| **1** | **2** | **3** | **4** | **5** |
|---|---|---|---|---|
| A | B | C | D | E |
| J | K | L | M | N |
| S | T | U | V | W |

| **6** | **7** | **8** | **9** |
|---|---|---|---|
| F | G | H | I |
| O | P | Q | R |
| X | Y | Z | |

# Single Numbers

**Number 1**
(*Those born on 1st, 10th, 19th, 28th of any month*)
1. Creative.
2. Strong.
3. Obstinate.
4. Inventive.
5. Determined.
6. Definite in views.
7. Ambitious individual.
8. Dislikes restraint.
9. Successful in profession.
10. Has leadership qualities.

*Lucky Colours* : All shades of gold, yellow and bronze.

*Lucky Days* : Sunday and Monday.

*Lucky Gems* : Topaz, amber and yellow diamond.

**Number 2**
*(2nd, 11th, 20th, 29th)*
1. Imaginative.
2. Artistic and romantic.
3. Gentle and modest.
4. Restless and unsettled.
5. Oversensitive.
6. Lacks self-confidence.
7. Easily despondent.
8. Cooperative and friendly.

9. Diplomatic and arbitrary.
10. Adaptable.
11. Modest and gracious.

*Lucky Colours* : All shades of green, cream and white.

*Lucky Days* : Sunday, Monday and Friday.

*Lucky Gems* : Pearl, moonstone and jade.

**Number 3**
*(3rd, 12th, 21st, 30th)*
1. Ambitious.
2. Very independent.
3. Proud.
4. Dictatorial.

5. Desirous of authority.
6. Conscientious.
7. Cheerful and happy.
8. Artistic and creative.
9. Imaginative and inspiring.
10. Versatile and brilliant.
11. Optimistic.

*Lucky Colours* : Mauve, violet and purple.

*Lucky Days* : Thursday, Friday and Tuesday.

*Lucky Gem* : Amethyst.

**Number 4**
*(4th, 13th, 22nd, 31st)*
1. Cautious and deliberative.

2. Rebellious and determined.
3. Very positive and practical.
4. Sensitive.
5. Highly strung and sensitive.
6. Given to deep despondency.
7. Industrious and responsible.
8. Systematic and orderly.
9. Steady and efficient.
10. Faithful bent of mind.
11. Scientific bent of mind.

*Lucky Colours* : Half shades, electric blue and greys.

*Lucky Days* : Saturday, Sunday and Monday.

*Lucky Gem* : Sapphire.

# Number 5

*(5th, 14th, 23rd)*

1. Friendly.
2. Impulsive.
3. Energetic.
4. Clever.
5. Action-oriented.
6. Irritable and quick-tempered.
7. Loves gambling and speculation.
8. Quick in thought and decision.
9. Versatile and resourceful.
10. Loves freedom and amusement.

*Lucky Colours* : All shades of grey, white or light shades.

*Lucky Days* : Wednesday and Friday.

*Lucky Gems* : Diamond, platinum and silver.

## Number 6
*(6th, 15th, 24th)*
1. Friendly and generous.
2. Artistic and musical.
3. Magnetic and attractive.
4. Loveable and adorable.
5. Determined.
6. Responsible and righteous.
7. Obstinate.
8. Humane and just.
9. Loyal and dependable.
10. Fixed views.
11. Balanced and harmonious.

*Lucky Colours* : All shades of blue and pink.

*Lucky Days* : Tuesday, Thursday and Friday.

*Lucky Gems* : Turquoise and emerald.

**Number 7**
*(7th, 16th, 25th)*
1. Very independent.
2. Original and analytical.
3. Loves change and travel.
4. Restless.
5. A dreamer and mystic.
6. Dignified and understanding.
7. Investigative and observant.
8. Knowledgeable and intellectual.

9. Philosophical and clairvoyant.
10. Magnetic and charming.
11. Versatile, artistic and poetic.

*Lucky Colours* : All shades of green, pale shades, white and yellow.

*Lucky Days* : Sunday and Monday.

*Lucky Gems* : Cat's eye and pearls.

**Number 8**
*(8th, 17th, 26th)*
1. Philosophical.
2. Religious.
3. Wayward.
4. Sacrificing.
5. Deep and intense.
6. Kind and dependable.

7. Zealous and ambitious.
8. Fatalistic and fanatical.
9. Tough and tenacious.
10. Authoritative and efficient.

*Lucky Colours* : All shades of grey, black, dark blue and purple.

*Lucky Days* : Tuesday, Thursday and Friday.

*Lucky Gems* : Amethyst, dark sapphire and black pearl.

**Number 9**
*(9th, 18th, 27th)*
1. Impulsive.
2. Courageous.
3. Broad-minded.

4. Short-tempered.
5. Independent and selfless.
6. Affecionate, sympathetic and forgiving.
7. Gritty, strong-willed and determined.
8. Humane and compassionate.
9. Generous and charitable.
10. Philanthropic and spiritual.
11. Artistic and aesthetic.

*Lucky Colours* : All shades of crimson or red, and pink.

*Lucky Days* : Tuesday, Thursday and Friday.

*Lucky Gems* : Ruby, garnet and bloodstone.

# Compound and Karmic Numbers

When the total *value* of a person's name combined with his date of birth is taken as a whole, and not reduced to a single number, it is known as a compound number.

*e.g.* S   u   m   a   n
    1   3   4   1   5
    = 14

    K   u   m   a   r
    2   3   4   1   9
    = 19

```
D   a   t   t   a
4   1   2   2   1
= 10
```

14+19+10 = 43 **Compound No.**

Karmic numbers are special numbers which are never reduced to a single number. These numbers are:

*e.g.* 11, 13, 14, 16, 19, 22, 33, 44, 55, 61 and 63.

```
e.g. S   a   n   j   e   e   v
     1   1   5   1   5   5   4
     = 22
```

D i v a n j i
4 9 4 1 5 1 9
= 3 3

K a p u r

2 1 7 3 9

= 2 2

1. As a major number, the Compound or Karmic number has a lifelong effect, while as an Event number (see page 113), it is for a specific period.
2. 'Karma' stands for the result of one's action, and a karmic number in one's life denotes

repeated failures.
3. If it appears as an Event number, the ill-effects remain only for that particular period.
4. Once the Karmic number has lapsed, the individual emerges as a new being with greater potentials.

**Number 10**
1. Honourable.
2. Faithful.
3. Self-confident.
4. Fortunate.
5. Either successful or a failure.

## Number 11 (Karmic)
1. Humanitarian.
2. Energetic.
3. Intuitive and clairvoyant.
4. Prophetic ability.
5. Illuminating.
6. Warm-hearted.
7. Emotionally cool.

## Number 12
1. Atoning nature.
2. Suffers in silence.
3. Anxious and nervous.
4. Sacrificing.

## Number 13 (Karmic)
1. Faces life courageously.

2. Changes plans and places often.

## Number 14 (Karmic)
1. Sexual and energetic.
2. Indecisive and temperamental.
3. Ignorant and forgetful.
4. Mobile and enthusiastic.
5. Open to risk and danger.
6. Affectionate and loving.

## Number 15
1. Eloquent.
2. Sensuous.
3. Artistic.
4. Magnetic.
5. Sociable.
6. Musical.

## Number 16 (Karmic)
1. Weak-minded.
2. Subversive.
3. Danger of failures.

## Number 17
1. Forceful.
2. Independent.
3. Truthful.
4. Faithful and full of hope.
5. Has executive ability.
6. Balanced and intuitive.

## Number 18
1. Philanthropic.
2. Authoritative.
3. Quarrelsome.

4. Just and truthful.
5. Materialistic.
6. Extreme in nature.
7. Healing powers.

## Number 19 (Karmic)
1. Fortunate.
2. Successful.
3. Extremely favourable.
4. Esteemed and honoured.

## Number 20
1. Peace-loving.
2. Happy.
3. Spiritual.

## Number 21
1. Emotionally unstable.
2. Confused.
3. Poetic and literary.
4. Happy-go-lucky.
5. Wise and loving.
6. Successful.
7. Artistic and musical.
8. Generous and impulsive.
9. Honoured and powerful.

## Number 22 (Karmic)
1. Very capable.
2. Wise and intellectual.
3. Spiritual.
4. Creative.

5. Kind and sincere.
6. Humorous.

**Number 23**
1. Creative.
2. Considerate.
3. Successful and famous.
4. Clever and quick-thinking.
5. Gifted in speech and writing
6. Most fortunate.
7. Unselfish.
8. Daring.

**Number 24**
1. Artistic and creative.
2. Humane and just.
3. Loyal and dependable.

4. Harmonious and balanced.
5. Generous.
6. Love of domestic life.

**Number 25**
1. Successful.
2. Scientific bent of mind.
3. Love of freedom.
4. Philosophical and intuitive.
5. Observant.

**Number 26**
1. Diplomatic.
2. Self-indulgent.
3. Neglectful.
4. Prosperous.
5. Emotionally unbalanced.

6. Experienced and wise.
7. Energetic and compelling.
8. Leadership qualities.

**Number 27**
1. Wealthy.
2. Travels frequently.
3. Independent.
4. Literary.
5. Bigoted.
6. Love of art, beauty, peace and justice.
7. Creative.
8. Intellectual.
9. Intolerant.
10. Powerful and successful.
11. Quick-thinking.

## Number 28
1. Courageous.
2. An achiever.
3. Initiative.
4. Obstinate.
5. Original and individualistic.
6. Egoistic and boastful.
7. Creative and inventive.
8. Possesses leadership qualities.
9. Strong-willed and determined.
10. Humorous and witty.

## Number 29
1. Vulnerable.
2. Intuitive.
3. Scientific and religious.
4. Nervous and high-strung.

5. Warm-hearted and humane.
6. Artistic and musical.

**Number 30**
1. Highly emotional.
2. Impulsive.
3. Positive mental outlook.
4. Love of music and theatre.

**Number 31**
1. Selfish.
2. Self-contained.
3. Lonely.

**Number 32**
1. Creative.
2. Oratory skills.

3. Action-oriented.
4. Friendly and sociable.
5. Confederate and selfless.

## Number 33 (Karmic)
1. Steady and reliable.
2. Regular.
3. Dignified.
4. Discriminating.
5. Conservative.
6. Protective.
7. Considerate.

## Number 34
1. Creative.
2. Intuitive.

3. Religious and spiritual.
4. Retiring.
5. Conventional.

**Number 35**
1. Sometimes cruel.
2. Peaceful.
3. Enjoys travel.
4. Creative and successful.
5. Generally friendly.
6. Helpful.

**Number 36**
1. Creative.
2. Humane.
3. Influential.
4. Authoritative and powerful.

5. Kind and generous.
6. Sympathetic and helpful.

**Number 37**
1. Friendly.
2. Loving and generous.
3. Attractive.

**Number 38**
1. Not fortunate.
2. Spiritually powerful.
3. Nervous and unstable.

**Number 39**
1. Healthy and blessed with long life.
2. Friendly and loving.

## Number 40
1. Economic.
2. Selfless and generous.
3. Mathematically talented.
4. Easy-going and relaxed.

## Number 41
1. Successful.
2. In control of passions.
3. Achiever.

## Number 42
1. Strongly religious.
2. Very helpful.
3. Artistic and musical.
4. Can be treacherous.

## Number 43
1. Faced with calamities.
2. Failures possible.
3. Possible dangers.

## Number 44 (Karmic)
1. Brave.
2. Successful and glorious.
3. Personal losses may accrue.

## Number 45
1. Helpful.
2. Mentally alert.
3. Good marital life.

## Number 46
1. Inventive.

2. Psychic.
3. Scientific.
4. Idealist.
5. Ambitious.
6. Quick-tempered.

## Number 47
1. Unstable.
2. Cooperative.
3. Discriminating.
4. Agreeable and tactful.

## Number 48
1. Affectionate.
2. Pleasure-loving.
3. Successful.
4. Psychic.

5. Sociable.
6. Happy marriage.
7. Artistic.
8. Self-indulgent.

**Number 49**
1. Well-balanced.
2. Spiritual.
3. Egoistic.
4. Diplomatic.
5. Virtuous.
6. Insincere.

**Number 50**
1. Very active.
2. Eloquent.
3. Magnetic.

4. Dominating.
5. Successful and renowned.
6. Famous.
7. Powerful.
8. Leadership qualities.

**Number 51**
1. Leadership qualities.
2. Successful.
3. Powerful.
4. Cheerful.

**Number 52**
1. Patient.
2. Love of nature.
3. Courageous.
4. Spiritual.

## Number 53
1. Analytical.
2. Authoritative.
3. Temperamental.
4. Set in ways.

## Number 54
1. Eloquent.
2. Healthy.
3. Respected.
4. Longevity.
5. Wealthy.

## Number 55 (Karmic)
1. Dominating.
2. Religious.
3. Sharp.

4. Enthusiastic.
5. Leadership qualities.
6. Honest.
7. Inspiring.

**Number 56**
1. Dominating.
2. Gains fortune.
3. Ambitious.
4. Inspiring.
5. Achieves great distinction.
6. Nervous and restless.

**Number 57**
1. Pleasant.
2. Active.
3. Healthy.

4. Sociable.
5. Exhibitionist.
6. Prosperous and successful.

**Number 58**
1. Healthy.
2. Affectionate.
3. Occultist.
4. Frank.
5. Fickle-minded.

**Number 59**
1. Successful with marine ventures.
2. Speculating and gambling nature.

3. Swindling and fraudulent tendencies.

**Number 60**
1. Cheerful.
2. Healthy.
3. A rebel.
4. Insubordinate.

**Number 61 (Karmic)**
1. Sincere.
2. Self-controlled.
3. Fond of pleasures.
4. Peaceful.
5. Travels.

## Number 62
1. Deeply intensive.
2. Ambitious.
3. Wayward.
4. Individualistic.
5. Philosophical.

## Number 63 (Karmic)
1. Reformer.
2. Wasteful.
3. Healthy.
4. A drifter.

## Number 64
1. Literary.
2. Individualistic.
3. Makes most of opportunities.

## Number 65
1. Spiritual.
2. Happy marital life.
3. Religious

# The Destiny Number

1. Reduce each part of your name to a single digit.

*e.g.*   S   u   m   a   n
    1   3   4   1   5  = 14

    K   u   m   a   r
    2   3   4   1   9  = 19

    D   a   t   t   a
    4   1   2   2   1  = 10

14 + 19 + 10

1+4=5   1+9=10   1+0=1

1+0=1

2. Then find the grand total by adding the values of all the names, reducing it to a single digit, which becomes your destiny number.

*e.g.*     Suman   Kumar   Datta
         5        1       1   =   $\boxed{7}$
                               **Destiny No.**

3. Two karmic numbers 11 and 22 are not reduced since they have their own powers.
4. Each part of your name has its own influence :

   *First name*: represents the personal side of nature.

*Second name*: represents the reserved forces called upon when necessary.

*Third or family name*: represents the characteristics and hereditary influence of the family on one.

5. A person may have one, two or even four names, but it is the destiny number eventually which becomes important.

**Number 1**
1. A leader in one's field of work.
2. Should rely on one's own abilities.

3. Should be courageous and determined.
4. Will be an outstanding person.
5. Should shed egoism.

**Number 2**
1. Cooperation and association will result in success.
2. Diplomatic and peaceful.
3. Partnership will be beneficial.

**Number 3**
1. Popular.
2. Romantic and loving.
3. Happy, cheerful and a joy - giver.

4. Imaginative and creative.
5. Sincere.

**Number 4**
1. Shoulders responsibilities.
2. Construction, organisation and management will be the main occupation.
3. Patient and determined.
4. Honest and sincere.

**Number 5**
1. Born to promote freedom and progress.
2. Frequent changes in circumstances and approaches.
3. Versatile.

**Number 6**
1. Service with love and responsibility.
2. Charitable and dependable.
3. Love, comfort and money assured by helping others.
4. Beauty, companionship, love and harmony needed for progress.
5. Philosophical and spiritual.

**Number 7**
1. Scientific.
2. Philosophical and religious.
3. Sense of loneliness.

4. Popularity, love and respect achieved due to knowledge attained.
5. An educator.
6. Personal business, love and marriage may be secondary.

**Number 8**
1. Authority and recognition assured.
2. Philosophical.
3. Famous in the line of business.

**Number 9**
1. Philanthropic and spiritual.
2. Humanitarian and compassionate.

3. Charitable and generous.
4. Deep interest in art and romance.
5. Popular, but selfish and personal love could bring disappointments.

**Number 11**

1. Inspiration, spiritual awareness, intuition and psychic powers will bring happiness.
2. Destined to achieve higher values of life.
3. Chances of material loss.
4. Sensitive, nervous and self-centred.

**Number 22**
1. A position of authority.
2. Spiritually aware.
3. Can be famous through psychic and mystic revelations.

# The Talent Number

1. The sum total of the month, date of birth and year is the Talent Number.

*e.g.* J a n u a r y

1 1 5 3 1 9 7 = 27 = 9

10    =   1

1948  =  22 = 4

9 + 1 + 4 = 14 = $\boxed{5}$ **Talent No.**

2. The Talent number remains constant, with no changes in life.
3. This number reveals the individual's natural potency, talents and characteristics, and also the positive and negative aspects.
4. The Talent number is the tool in hand, while the Destiny number is the work that needs to be accomplished, and much depends on their harmonious union.
5. Having a Karmic number as the Talent number denotes difficulties in life.

6. One's Talent and Destiny numbers together reveal our succeses and failures.

*e.g.* Suman Kumar Datta
       5       1       1 =7 **Destiny**

January 10 1948
       9     1     4       =5 **Talent**

Suman will be popular, loved and respected for the knowledge attained in the scientific, philosophical or religious field, but drinking excessively, and moving from one activity to another restlessly may result in a setback.

# The Heart Number

1. The sum total of all the vowels in one's full name, reduced to a single digit, is the Heart number.

*e.g.* S u m a n
     3    1    = 4

K u m a r
   3    1    = 4

D u t t a
   1      1  = 2

4 + 4 + 2 = 10

1 + 0 = $\boxed{1}$ **Heart No.**

2. Karmic numbers 11 and 22 are not reduced to single numbers.
3. The Heart number represents a person's desires which certainly have a bearing on other major numbers.

**Number 1**
1. Independent.
2. Determined.
3. Initiative.
4. Honest.
5. Ambitious.
6. Executive ability.
7. Leadership qualities.
8. Hates subordination.

## Number 2
1. Cooperative.
2. Diplomatic.
3. Loving.
4. Spiritual.
5. Sincere.
6. Friendly.
7. Loves company.
8. Harmonious.

## Number 3
1. Imaginative.
2. Outgoing.
3. Artistic.
4. Extravagant.
5. Full of inspiration.

6. Talkative.
7. Very loving.
8. Easy-going.

**Number 4**
1. Result-oriented.
2. Responsible.
3. Constructive.
4. Practical.
5. Reliable and honest.
6. Tensed.

**Number 5**
1. Versatile.
2. Resourceful.
3. Loves to get involved in public dealings.

4. Frequent changes in everything.
5. Seeks freedom and excitement.
6. Progressive.

## Number 6
1. Harmonious.
2. Responsible.
3. Humane.
4. Home-loving.
5. Craves for beauty, love and companionship.
6. Sympathetic.
7. Sacrificing.
8. Marital happiness.
9. Emotional.

## Number 7
1. Perfectionist.
2. Scientific.
3. A romantic.
4. Strong likes and dislikes.
5. Religious.
6. Meditative.

## Number 8
1. Materialistic.
2. Executive ability.
3. Accomplishing.
4. Psychic.
5. Too exacting.
6. Stubborn.
7. A good organiser.
8. Loves power and wealth.

9. Business-like approach.
10. Philosophical.
11. Dominating.

**Number 9**
1. Impersonal.
2. Forgiving.
3. Generous.
4. Religious.
5. Impressionable.
6. Helpful.
7. Compassionate.
8. Intuitive.
9. Whimsical.
10. Moody.

## Number 11
1. Intuitive.
2. Spiritual.
3. Aesthetic.
4. Helpful.
5. Sensitive.
6. Inspirational.
7. Sacrificing.
8. A perfectionist.
9. Potential for religious heights.
10. Nervous and tense.

## Number 22
1. Practical.
2. Respected.
3. Nervous and tense.

4. Perceptive and aware.
5. Achieves good position.

# The Birth Force Period

1. A person's life is divided into three periods during which subtle forces of nature influence his development, progress and retirement in life.
2. The first period is influenced by the number of the month of birth, the second, by the number of the day of birth, and the third, by the year of birth, each reduced to a single or master digit.

3. The first period is from birth to 25 or 26 years, the second lasts till 50 or 52 years, and the third, till the end of one's life.
4. The transition from one period to another takes a couple of years, with the influence of the last 2 or 3 years of one period tapering off and the first 2 or 3 years of the next period starting.

**Number 1**
*First Period*
1. Independent.
2. Individualistic.
3. Original.

*Second Period*
1. Positive approach.
2. Achiever.
3. Original.
4. Recognition in life.

*Third Period*
1. Attainment of success.
2. Recognition in life.

**Number 2**

*First Period*
1. Difficulty in development of faculties.
2. Weak in expression.

*Second Period*
1. Cooperative.

2. Partnership success.
3. Diplomatic.
4. Harmony in life.

*Third Period*
1. Happy domestic life.
2. Spiritual.
3. Social life salient.
4. Non-demanding.

## Number 3

*First Period*
1. Happy.
2. Imaginative.
3. Artistic.
4. A wastrel at times.
5. Optimistic.
6. Creative.

7. Extravagant.

*Second Period*
1. Self-expressive.
2. Enjoys pleasures of life and is self-indulgent.
3. Imaginative.

*Third Period*
1. Happy.
2. Social.
3. Cheerful.

**Number 4**

*First Period*
1. Practical.
2. Systematic and orderly.
3. Frustration due to limitation of money.

*Second period*
1. Practical.
2. Ambitious.
3. Frustrated due to shortage of money.
4. Productive.
5. Sincere.

*Third Period*
1. Serves humanity.
2. Workaholic.
3. Frustrated.

**Number 5**

*First Period*
1. Versatile.
2. Restlessness.
3. Free and creative.

4. Lack of money.

*Second Period*
1. Achieves fame.
2. Disappointments.
3. Over-indulgence in pleasures and sex.
4. Adaptable to changes.

*Third Period*
1. Active.
2. Tries to improve monetary conditions.
3. Love of pleasure.

**Number 6**
*First Period*
1. Responsible.

2. Serves others.
3. Loving.
4. Sacrificing.
5. Love of domestic life.
6. Early marriage.

*Second Period*
1. Balanced.
2. Home-loving.
3. Loving.
4. Responsible.

*Third Period*
1. Friendly.
2. Responsible.
3. Domestic.
4. Helpful.

## Number 7

*First Period*
1. Analytical.
2. Detached.
3. High concentration.

*Second Period*
1. Analytical and research-oriented.
2. Skilled or specialised work may be accomplished.
3. Selective and a perfectionist.

*Third Period*
1. Studious.
2. Might achieve spiritual perfection.

## Number 8

*First Period*
1. Authoritative.
2. Materialistic.
3. Powerful.

*Second Period*
1. Ability for administration.
2. Sound judgement.
3. A progressive period with time to relax.

*Third Period*
1. Continues working.
2. Practical.

## Number 9

*First Period*
1. Emotional.
2. Dissatisfied.
3. Selfish.

*Second Period*
1. Philanthropic.
2. Impersonal.
3. Selfless.
4. Neglect of personal life.

*Third Period*
1. Quiet.
2. Dissatisfied personal life.
3. Selfless service.

## Number 11

*First Period*
1. Philosophical.
2. Religious.

*Second Period*
1. Spiritual or philosophical activities.
2. Unconcerned with business or materialistic things.

*Third Period*
1. Quiet.
2. Philosophical.
3. Religious.

## Number 22

*First Period*

1. A smooth, progressive life.

*Second Period*

1. Spiritual aspect develops.
2. Interested in handling big projects.

*Third Period*

1. Continues to work and unfailing interest in projects continues.

# The Ultimate Number

1. The sum of the Destiny and Talent numbers, reduced to a single digit, is called the Ultimate number.

*e.g.* Suman Kumar Datta
    5     1      1   = 7
                          **Destiny**

January 10 1948
   9    1    4   = 5
                    **Talent**

7 + 5 = 12 = $\boxed{3}$
                    **Ultimate**

2. This number represents the ultimate goal in life, around which all activities revolve.
3. It is also known as the Reality number, Power number or Maturity number.
4. In the early part of one's life, its effect is quite markedly noticeable, and later on, it goes into the subconscious from where it affects life.
5. While young, when the person is concerned with matters of immediate interest and results, he should utilise this opportunity to fulfil his dream

to make his later days worthwhile.

6. If it happens to be the same number as any of the major numbers, then the activities and their benefits are enhanced or reduced.
7. As a new number, its effect is experienced suddenly, sometimes making circumstances very uncomfortable.
8. As a Karmic number, it creates obstacles.

**Number 1**
1. Individualistic.
2. Original.

3. Separation from spouse possible.
4. Very independent.
5. Leadership qualities.

**Number 2**
1. Diplomatic.
2. Successful.
3. Spiritually aware.
4. Sensitive.
5. Cooperative.
6. Practical.

**Number 3**
1. Self-expressive.
2. Imaginative.

3. Creative.
4. Self-indulgent.

## Number 4
1. Limitations and restrictions.
2. Tenacious.
3. Disciplined.
4. Chances of a broken marriage or business ruin.

## Number 5
1. Freedom and opportunities.
2. Over-indulgence of sex.
3. Broken marriage likely.
4. Travels frequently.
5. Benefits from opportunities.

## Number 6
1. Dutiful.
2. Loving.
3. Comforts.
4. Responsible.
5. Humane.
6. Love and protection assured.

## Number 7
1. Retiring.
2. Love of solitude.
3. Intuitive.
4. Philosophical.
5. Spiritual.
6. Contemplative.
7. Intellectual and wise.
8. Peaceful.

9. Enlightening others.
10. Indifferent and self-centred.

**Number 8**
1. Materialistic.
2. Disciplined.
3. Commands respect.
4. Determined.
5. Executive ability.
6. Loves power and position.

**Number 9**
1. Philanthropic.
2. Loving and giving.
3. Helpful and compassionate.
4. Spiritually aware.

5. Selfish and dissatisfied sometimes.

**Number 11**
1. Spiritual.
2. Simple living.
3. Not interested in material things.
4. Cooperative.

**Number 22**
1. Recognition in life.
2. Worldly possessions.
3. Interested in materialistic gains.
4. Idealistic.
5. Helpful.

# The Challenge Number

1. To get the challenge number, find the difference between the month and day digits, then between the day and year digits, then between the first and second remainders found above, and finally between the month and year digits.

*e.g.*    January    10    1948

             9       1       4

                8      3

**5/5 Challenge Number**

The difference between month and date = 9 - 1 = 8

The difference between date and year = 1 - 4 = 3

The difference between 1st and 2nd remainders = 8 - 3 = 5

The difference between month and year = 9 - 4 = 5

2. In the beginning of life, the challenge number shows the negative aspects of the concerned number, and if these are overcome, then opportunities for growth and accomplishment are assured.

## Number 1
1. Dominated by others.
2. Resentful.
3. Opposition in life.
4. Headstrong.

## Number 2
1. Shy and timid.
2. Fearful.
3. Harmonious.
4. Cooperative.
5. Perfectionist.
6. Lacks self-confidence.
7. Feeling of subordination.
8. Intelligent and sensitive.

## Number 3
1. Imaginative and creative.
2. Shy and fears repression.
3. Popular and successful in romance, arts, writing.
4. Gift of words and speech.
5. Optimistic.

## Number 4
1. Careless and rigid.
2. Impractical.
3. Can accomplish marvels with talents as a holder with hidden ideas and concepts.
4. Impatient.
5. Indolent.

## Number 5
1. Restless.
2. Impatient.
3. Irresponsible.
4. Over-indulgence in worldly pleasures.
5. Constructive.
6. Restful.
7. Versatile.

## Number 6
1. Dominating.
2. High standards.
3. Self-righteous.
4. Appreciative.
5. Happy domestic life.
6. Irresponsible.

7. Intolerant.
8. Humane and tender.
9. Impersonal.

**Number 7**
1. Reserved and lonely.
2. Analytical.
3. Should have faith in his abilities.
4. Can accomplish marvels in technology, the occult, and education.
5. Very proud.
6. Understanding.

**Number 8**
1. Materialistic.
2. Opposition to proposals.

3. Philosophical and shrewd.
4. Power and authority.
5. Frustrated.

**Number 9**
1. Tolerant.
2. Forgiving.
3. Philanthropic.
4. Feeling of emptiness in life.
5. Loving and warm.

# The Personality Number

1. When all the consonants in one's name are added, and reduced to a single number, you get the personality number.

*e.g.*  S u m a n
    1        4     5 = 10

K u m a r
2    4    9 = 15

D a t t a
4    2   2     = 8

10 + 15 + 8 = 33

= ⬛6⬛ **Personality**

## Number 1
1. Dignified.
2. Well-dressed.
3. Outstanding.
4. Impressive.

## Number 2
1. Pleasing.
2. Love of details.
3. Stylish and well-dressed.
4. Gentle.
5. Fussy.

## Number 3
1. Talkative.
2. Artistic.
3. Showy.

4. Friendly.
5. Love of clothes and jewellery.

**Number 4**
1. Serious.
2. Neatly dressed.
3. Practical.

**Number 5**
1. Ultra-modern.
2. Talkative.
3. Boastful.

**Number 6**
1. Sympathetic.
2. Shabbily dressed.
3. Compassionate.

## Number 7
1. Charming.
2. Friendly and likeable.
3. Reserved in one's talk.
4. Impressive manners.

## Number 8
1. Showy and dressy.
2. Friendly.
3. Optimistic.

## Number 9
1. Friendly and warm.
2. Young-looking.
3. Pleasing manners.
4. Whimsical.
5. Generous.

6. Successful.
7. Magnetic personality.
8. Energetic
9. Optimistic
10. Healthy and robust

# The Birthday Number

Those born on:

*1st, 10th, 19th, 28th*
Having an additional force of will, determination and individuality, with those born on 19th probably having to face difficulties.

*2nd, 11th, 20th, 29th*
Sympathetic, cooperative and diplomatic, with those born on 11th and 29th also being psychic or spiritual but suffering from nerves.

*3rd, 12th, 21st, 30th*
Creative, artistive, optimistic and talented.

*4th, 13th, 22nd, 31st*
Practical and hard-working, with 13th born being frustrated frequently.

*5th, 14th, 23rd*
Versatile, quick, clever, enjoying food, drink and sex, and shirking responsibilities at times.

*6th, 15th, 24th*
Artistic, generous, responsible, loving and interested in home and family.

*7th, 16th, 25th*
Analytical, preferring to be alone for rest or meditation, capable of high achievements.

*8th, 17th, 26th*
Materialistic, capable in business, ambitious, successful as organisers or administrators.

*9th, 18th, 27th*
Cooperative, tolerant, forgiving, creative, sympathetic, compassionate, philanthropic, humane and spiritual.

# The Name Number

1. This is the sum total of one's first name reduced to a single digit.
2. The Name number is studied in relation to the Destiny, Talent and Heart numbers.

*eg.*  S   u   m   a   n
     1   3   4   1   5 = 14 = 5
     K   u   m   a   r
     2   3   4   1   9 = 19 = 1
     D   a   t   t   a
     4   1   2   2   1 = 10 = 1

     5   1   1 = 7  **Destiny**

January 10, 1948

J a n u a r y
1 1 5 3 1 9 7
27 = 9

1 0
1 + 0 = 1

1 9 4 8
1 + 9 + 4 + 8
22 = 4

9 + 1 + 4 = 14 = 5  **Talent**

S u m a n
3     1
3 + 1 = 4

K u m a r
   3      1

$3 + 1 = 4$

D a t t a
   1      1

$1 + 1 = 2$

$4 + 4 + 2 = 10 = 1$ **Heart**

S u m a n
1 3 4 1 5

$= 14 = \boxed{5}$ **Name**

3. A dominating number 5, consolidates the Talent number 5, making the person more

energetic, resourceful, clever, entertaining and amusing, having a very philosophical outlook as the Destiny number denotes, whereas the Heart number shows the person as being egoistic.

# The Habit Number

1. The total number of letters in one's name represents the Habit number.

*e.g.* S u m a n
5

K u m a r
5

D a t t a
5

5 + 5 + 5 = 15

2. This number acts as a modifier of either positive or negative aspects in conjunction with the major number.

**First Letter Number**
1. The first letter of one's name represents the material viewpoint of the person.

*e.g.* The first letter of Suman being S (number 3), she is creative, imaginative, determined and independent.

2. This number will quietly function in achieving the

requirements of the major number.

**First Vowel Number**

1. The first vowel in one's name represents the inner or spiritual viewpoint of a person.
2. This number too helps in supplementing the needs of the major number.

*e.g.* The first vowel in Suman being U (number 3), it shows that she is warm-hearted, witty, and spreads joy around.

# The Event Number

1. The numerical values of the first letter of each name are added to give the event number.

*e.g.* S u m a n
1

K u m a r
2

D a t t a
2

1 + 2 + 2 = 5    **Event**

2. The numerical values of letters in each name are added, then reduced to single digits, representing the duration each name works repeatedly.

*e.g.* S u m a n
1 3 4 1 5
= 14

K u m a r
2 3 4 1 9
= 19

D a t t a
2 1 2 2 1
= 18

The first name, Suman, will be in force till the age of 14 years, the experience starts once again from 14 till 28, then till 42, and so on. Likewise, the second name influences till 19 years, the experience will be repeated in cycles of 19, and the third name similarly in cycles of 8.

3. The cumulative effect of all names is figured out for each year, giving the kind of event experienced in that year.

4. The numerical value of a letter denotes the nature and duration of the event.

*e.g.* The letter S in Suman has a value of 1 which denotes that the activities of number 1 will take place for a year whenever the letter S appears in life. From birth till 1 year of age, Suman is under the influence of number 1, then U with value 3 takes over for 3 years till she is 4, and so on.

**Number 1**
1. New contacts, ideas, and interest start developing.
2. Chances of recognition increases.
3. New occupation likely.

**Number 2**
1. Success through partnerships and group activities.
2. Diplomacy, cooperation and patience required.
3. Delays cause frustration.
4. Emotions and sensitivity should be controlled.

**Number 3**
1. Friendship, love affairs, social activities, pleasure and travel are indicated.
2. Hobbies involving creativity and imagination can become vocations.

3. Accomplishments result from optimism and enthusiasm.
4. Indulgence in pleasure will lead to disappointment and squandering away of a good period.

**Number 4**
1. Matters relating to home, business, finance and relatives need to be attended to.
2. Preoccupation with one's own health or someone else's.
3. Feeling of limitations or slow progress needs to be overcome.

**Number 5**
1. Sudden and unforeseen happenings and meeting with people result in favourable changes.
2. Excitement, travel, new contacts and freedom are ensured.
3. Restlessness needs to be curbed.

**Number 6**
1. Responsibility, domestic affairs, love and marriage are salient.
2. Beware of dishonesty and selfishness which can lend to disappointments, and even separation.

3. Responsibilities undertaken will lead to love and financial inheritance.
4. Social recognition and popularity through humanitarian service.

**Number 7**
1. Writing, research, introspection, meditation and search for inner peace are salient features.
2. Interested in religious, philosophical or metaphysical fields.
3. Remaining aloof, one can have psychic or intuitive flashes leading to spiritual awakening.

4. Marital problems likely.

**Number 8**
1. Power, position and recognition through hard work and good judgement.
2. Travel for business, publishing, advertisement, etc., is on the cards.
3. Love and marriage unhappy unless the partners have the same level of thinking and compatibility.
4. Selling and buying of property likely.

**Number 9**

1. Opportunities galore, but impersonal views and a high moral character are necessary for success.
2. Ending an experience or a personal relationship may be saddening but necessary for future progress.
3. Highly emotional, leading to several experiences in love and friendship.
4. Dishonesty may result in legal tangles.
5. Creativity, philanthropy and humanitarianism will bring in success.

6. Money, travel and comfort are assured, while extravagance and indulgence in rich food lead to health hazards.

# Opportunities and Vocations

The single number (see page 10) is considered for vocational opportunities.

**Number 1**
1. Leadership qualities leading to power and position.
2. Quickness in decisions and actions lead to people seeking guidance.
3. Engineers, writers, composers of music, teachers, designers, architects, planners, presidents

of societies, curators or librarians or keepers of departmental stores.

**Number 2**
1. With a fine sense of timing and rhythm, they collect details and bring unity and harmony.
2. Aesthetic, spiritual and responsibly completing a given task are their greatest plus points.
3. Doctors, pharmacists, electronic engineers, teachers, bankers, musicians, artists, designers, consultants, nurses, book-keepers, secretaries.

## Number 3

1. Being energetic, confident, talented, imaginative and ambitious, they are successful in all fields.
2. Success, money, travel are assured.
3. Musicians, artists, writers, designers, teachers, commentators, salesmen, occultists—in fact, they excel in all fields.

## Number 4

1. Being honest and concentrating on their work, they accomplish a lot.

2. They excel at arrangements, constructions and maintenance.
3. Engineers, educators, businessmen, farmers, scientists, manufacturers, professors, legal practitioners, keepers of stores or other establishments, builders.

**Number 5**
1. Being resourceful, versatile, quick-minded and capable, they achieve success easily.
2. Indulgence in wine, women and pleasures make them popular.
3. Public relations officers, sales executives, managers of tourism

or transportation, industrialists, organisers of games or entertainments, legal practitioners, any line of civics from a clerk to a judge, dramatists, reporters, administrators, gamblers, occultists, religionists, psychologists.

## Number 6

1. With their initiative, creativity, energy, intelligence and capability, they serve others humbly and bring harmony and love.
2. With a sense of responsibility, they execute all their duties

diligently, for they represent unity of body and soul.

3. Teachers, philosophers, educators, religionists, scientists, ministers, instructors, writers, producers of luxury and beauty goods, managers of restaurants or clubs or luxury apartments, irrigationists, horticulturists, zoologists, shipping magnates.

**Number 7**

1. Being intuitive, mentally aware, calm, serene, thoughtful and contemplative, wise and knowledgeable, he is sought for his wise counsel.

2. Though lonely even in the midst of a crowd, the person learns to live with his soul.
3. Skilled workers in any field, historians, philosophers, poets, writers, counsellors, advisers.

**Number 8**
1. Endowed with an eye for detail, awareness, power of judgement, capability of handling materialism, management skills, they serve mankind by providing growth, progress and knowledge in a balanced way.
2. Constantly struggling, they work very hard to achieve

success, finally becoming imprejudiced leaders.
3. Administrators, supervisors, industrialists, builders, politicians, printers, publishers, engineers, philosophers, social scientists, public speakers, leaders in commerce or travel and tourism.

**Number 9**
1. Possessing all the virtues of all the numbers from 1 to 8 they provide true service to mankind.
2. When they work for self with selfish motives, they experience pain and disappointment,

otherwise they radiate divine love.
3. Artists, dramatists, writers, actors, painters, designers, lecturers, religionists, composers, publishers, restaurateurs, entertainers, surgeons, tourism directors.

# Romance and Marriage

The single number (see page 10) is considered for romance and marriage.

**Number 1**
1. Desirous of deep love.
2. Egoistic, so appears cold.
3. Likes to dominate the family.

**Number 2**
1. Sweet and cooperative companion.
2. Will go to any lengths for a lasting companionship.

**Number 3**
1. Romantic.
2. Desirous of a give-and-take attitude.
3. Cannot forget a broken affair easily.

**Number 4**
1. Desires stability and security rather than romance.
2. Prefers his partner to share his responsibilities.
3. Sincere and dependable in love affairs.

### Number 5
1. Prefers the opposite sex more for pleasure than stability in marriage, love and home.
2. Seeks change and freedom.

### Number 6
1. Ideal companion in love, marriage and home.
2. Constantly seeks approval of the loved one.

### Number 7
1. Very selective in choosing mate.
2. Capable of deep love

### Number 8
1. Being materialistic, neglects marriage and romance.
2. Prefers mate to be capable, ambitious and strong.

### Number 9
1. Impressionable and compassionate in romance.
2. An impersonal and negligent attitude can lead to loss of the beloved.

### Number 11
1. Philanthropic and universal ideas make the person's love-life interesting.

2. The person can be romantic only if the mate is as philosophical or religious.
3. If the marriage clicks their love will be deep.

**Number 22**
1. Desirous of love with a high awareness.
2. Prefers the mate to help him in humanitarian service to mankind for a steady relationship.

# Numbers and Diseases

**Number 1**
1. Persons born on the 1st, 10th, 19th or 28th of any month, are generally afflicted with ailments of the heart, like skipping heartbeats, palpitations, high or low blood pressure, etc.
2. Eye complaints, like watery eyes, a burning sensation in the eyes, astigmatism, myopia, etc., might trouble one throughout one's life. It would be advisable

to regularly get the eyes checked.
3. In their nineteenth, twenty-eighth, thirty-seventh and forty-sixth, and fifty fifth years, changes in health will be obvious.
4. October, December and January are the months when ill-health might result due to overwork.
5. Citrus fruits, ginger, raisins, cloves, dates, bayleaves, thyme, nutmeg and saffron are some recommenced remedial cures against the above mentioned ailments.

## Number 2

1. Those born on the 2nd, 11th, 20th or 29th of any month suffer from disorders of the stomach and the digestive organs.
2. Important changes in health occur in their twentieth, twenty-fifth, twenty-ninth, forty-third, forty-seventh, fifty-second, and sixty-fifth years.
3. January, February and July are the months to be most guarded against ill-health and overwork.
4. Melon, lettuce, cucumber, cabbages and turnips prove beneficial to one's health.

# Number 3

1. Those born on the 3rd, 12th, 21st or 30th of any month are likely to suffer from nervous disorders brought about by strain and stress.
2. Neuritis and sciatica are also indicated in some.
3. Skin disorders might occur in a few.
4. December, February, June and September are the months to be guarded against overwork and ill-health.
5. Changes in health are indicated in their twelfth, twenty-first,

thirty-ninth, forty-eighth and fifty-seventh years.
6. Pineapples, grapes, pomegranates, peaches, apples, strawberries, cherries, mulberries, mint, saffron, mutmegs, cloves, almonds, figs, wheat and hazelnuts will be beneficial to one's health.

**Number 4**
1. Those born on the 4th, 13th, 22nd or 31st of any month are likely to suffer from ailments that are difficult to diagnose at once.

2. They have a tendency towards melancholia.
3. Anaemia can be a depressive or troublesome ailment.
4. Pains in the head and back are a recurring factor.
5. January, February, July, August and September are the months to be guarded against for ill-health and overwork.
6. The thirteenth, twenty-second, thirty-first, fortieth, forty-ninth and fifty-eighth years show changes in one's health.
7. Spinach is highly recommended as a curative measure against diseases.

8. Electric treatment, hypnotism and counselling about one's mental framework and suggestive remedial measures prove beneficial.

**Number 5**
1. All those born on the 5th, 14th or 23rd of a month are likely to suffer due to stress, affecting the nervous system.
2. They are mentally overworked, and prone to neuritis, insomnia and restlessness.
3. June, September and December can be harmful months for health.

4. The fourteenth, twenty-third, thirty-second, forty-first and fiftieth years depict changes in health.
5. Carrots, oats, parsley, caraway seeds, thyme, and nuts, especially hazelnuts and walnuts, are useful in combating diseases.

**Number 6**
1. Those born on the 6th, 15th or 24th are likely to suffer from afflictions of the throat, nose, and lungs, especially the upper part.

2. Constitutionally strong and robust, they will be healthy in an open countryside.
3. Women are prone to troubles of the breasts.
4. In advanced years, the heart might get affected.
5. Those born on the fifteenth twenty-fourth, thirty-third, forty-second, fifty-first and sixtieth years will see changes in their health.
6. May, October and November are the months to be guarded against.
7. Melons, apples, peaches, pomegranates, apricots, figs,

walnuts, almonds, beans, spinach, mint, thyme and parsnips are recommended for good health.

## Number 7

1. Those born on the 7th, 16th or 25th of any month are always irritable and snappy.
2. They tend to worry a lot and are pessimists.
3. They are extremely sensitive to their surroundings.
4. Being stronger mentally than physically, they undertake workload with which the body is unable to cope physically.

5. They have an extremely sensitive skin.
6. January, February, July and August are the months which can bring about a setback in their health.
7. The seventh, sixteenth, twenty-fifth, thirty-fourth, forty-third, fifty-second and sixty-first years show changes in health.
8. Apples, grapes, fruit-juices, cucumber, lettuce, cabbage, linseed, and mushrooms are recommended for better health.

## Number 8

1. Those born on the 8th, 17th or 26th are prone to problems connected with the liver and the intestines.
2. Frequent headaches can be another ailment.
3. Rheumatism can seriously affect one's health.
4. December, January, February and July are the months that may cause health problems.
5. The seventeenth, twenty-sixth, thirty-fifth, forty-fourth, fifty-third and sixty-second years bring about changes in health.

6. Bananas, marshmallows, carrots, spinach and celery are good for one's health.

**Number 9**
1. Those born on the 9th, 18th and 27th of any month are prone to fevers, measles, chickenpox, etc.
2. They would do better to avoid alcoholic drinks and rich food.
3. April, May, October and November are the months during which care of the health is necessary.
4. The ninth, eighteenth, twenty-seventh, thirty-sixth, forty-fifth and fifty-fourth years bring

about important changes in one's health.
5. Onions, garlic, leeks, mustard, ginger and pepper are good for one's general health.

# Numbers and Colours

**Number 1**
1. Those born on the 1st, 10th, 19th or 28th of any month would do well to use all shades of brown and yellow or gold colours.
2. Their dress should preferably in shades of yellow or brown, and gold ornaments enhance one's positive qualities.
3. Their bedroom can be any light shade of yellow.
4. The colours mentioned above will soothe their nerves, and

bring about harmony and a relaxed atmosphere.

**Number 2**
1. Those born on the 2nd, 11th, 20th or 29th of any month should use all shades of green, cream and white.
2. All light shades are preferable for clothes.
3. They should avoid all dark colours, especially black, purple and dark red.
4. Their bedroom can be either white or cream, or have light green walls.

5. These colours bring one mental peace and happiness.

**Number 3**
1. Those born on the 3rd, 12th, 21st or 30th of any month should use use colours in shades of mauve, violet, lilac or purple.
2. While ladies can use clothes of any of the above-mentioned colours, men can use neckties, shirts or handkerchiefs of these colours.
3. A lilac or mauve-washed wall in the bedroom would be ideal.
4. These colours enhance one's intuition and relax one's nerves.

## Number 4

1. Those born on the 4th, 13th, 22nd or 31st of any month should use electric colours, blues, greys, and half-shades.
2. Dreses in all shades of blues and greys, especially electric blue, bring out the person's inner beauty.
3. Strong or positive colours should be avoided.
4. A light-blue, or a pale grey ceiling or walls will be ideal for a person.
5. These colours bring out one's hidden talents, and help one to make rapid progress in life.

# Number 5

1. Those born on the 5th, 14th or 23rd should use light shades of all colours.
2. All clothes of light shades of grey and white, and made of glistening material would add grace to a person.
3. Dark colours should be avoided at all costs.
4. A room with light grey or white walls will bring contentment to a person.
5. These colours bring joy and prosperity to a person.

# Number 6

1. All those born on the 6th, 15th or 24th of any month should use colours of blue, besides pink.
2. Clothes in colour of blue, ranging from cerulean an blue to dark navy blue bring out the person's personality.
3. Shades of pink or rose mingled with tinges of blue can be used in clothes or jewellery.
4. Light blue walls in the bedroom give relaxation.
5. The various shades of blue enhance one's magnetic charm.

## Number 7

1. All those born on the 7th, 16th or 25th of any month should use all shades of pale green, white, yellow and gold colours.
2. Clothes in pastel shades add beauty to one's personality.
3. Pale-green, white or pale-yellow walls of the bedroom ensure relaxation.
4. The pastel shades enhance one's calm nature, and bring relief to one's stressed life.

## Number 8

1. Those born on the 8th, 17th or 26th of any month should use all

shades of dark grey, dark blue, purple and black.
2. Gaudy colours should be avoided.
3. A bedroom with light grey or blue walls soothe frayed nerves.
4. These colours enhance one's mental faculties.

**Number 9**
1. Those born on the 9th, 18th or 27th of any month should use all shades of red, crimson, pink and purple.
2. Darker shades of clothes are preferable to lighter ones.

3. Walls of a pale-pink colour in the bedroom bring a lot of peace to the person.
4. One's energies get enhanced on using these colours.